Cricut Mastery

How To Master Your Cricut
Machine, Project Ideas And The
Secrets To Get The Best Out Of
Cricut Design Space

Kelly J. White

Table Of Contents

Introduction

Thank you for purchasing this book.

The only limitation in using the Cricut is your imagination. Download this book now to learn more about this amazing machine and how to design a variety of craft projects. If you want to make creative use of your time, this book is exactly for you. In a world filled with bulk, handcrafted and ingenious factory-made products, design is sought after in the market. Personalized items are fast becoming a trend. Take advantage of this market and profit from your skills. You can explore a different number of products that can be made and sold using a Cricut Maker. Among them are custom shirts, vinyl crafts, kitchen items, mats, table runners, wine bottle holders and other things.

Enjoy

CHAPTER 1

PROJECTS WITH CRICUT MAKER—PROJECTS FOR BEGINNERS

Fruity Tray

Materials:

- An octagonal tray, crealia coral, light yellow, white, and leaf green decorative paints.
- One or two flat brushes.
- A pencil.
- A 10cm paper disc and brown.
- Black and glitter green poscas.
- Polish glue to varnish spray and masking tape.

Steps:

1. Draw disks on your board and paint them green (mix leaf green with light yellow). It will be necessary to make two layers. After drying, make yellow ovals in the center (light yellow and white) and paint in two coats. All this can be done using the Cricut template.

2. Trace the outlines of the discs in brown. Draw the green lines (see photo) in the green area and then the pips. Apply a spray varnish to prevent the posca from drooling in the glue varnish in the next step.

3. Stick the stickers with the varnish glue at the bottom of the tray. After drying, apply a little varnish in spray to prevent the ink of the stickers from dissolving in contact with the resin.

4. Using a glue gun, attach the small wooden fruit decorations.

Here are some indications for a successful resin:

1. First of all, the bottom of the tray must be varnished to prevent inks/colors/paints from bleeding into the paint. It is not systematic, but it could happen, so you better take the lead.
2. Then, respect the dosages of the packaging and check that you pour the hardener first.
3. Mix for a long time—10 minutes minimum per cup. Here there are two cups. I have mixed over 20 minutes. Don't hesitate to transfer your mixture to a new cup and mix it again.
4. Pour the resin in the center of the tray and distribute the whole by tilting it.
5. Let dry for two days, even if the packaging says 24h.

Craft Paper Pencil Holder

Materials:

- Imitation leathercraft paper braiding tape 9.5 cm.
- Self-healing cutting mat 60x45 cm.
- Transparent ruler for creative hobbies 40 cm.
- Scissors.
- Mini high-temperature glue gun.
- Pencil.
- Salvaged cardboard, glass, and jar or compass.

Steps:

1. Begin by taking a glass and a jar with different diameters. Then you need to trace the outlines of the circles on recycled cardboard. You may also cut it with a cutter. In addition to this, you need to know more about it.

2. Glue the cardboard discs together with the glue gun. Cut strips of craft paper braiding 20 cm long. Glue them one by one in radiation. Superimpose them slightly at the base: the bands must be the edge to edge at the circumference of the cardboard disc. In addition to this, you need to know more about it.

3. Cover the larger cardboard disc in this way. Glue with a glue gun. Fold the braiding strips, measure the cardboard disc's circumference, and cut five braiding strips of this size. In addition to this, you need to know more about it.

4. Slide a strip of braiding perpendicular under one of those welded to the cardboard base. Stick one end to it, as close as possible to the base. Pass it alternately under one vertical strip and over the next one. Attach a dot of glue to the glue gun under a few vertical stripes.

5. To close, glue the second end of the strip under the first end. In the same way, slip the second strip of braiding, mount a second row, tightening to avoid gaping spaces.

6. Set up the braiding of the pot with five strips in all. Fold a base strip towards the inside of the pot. Mark the fold in the pot to

mark the length. Cut off the excess. In addition to this, you need to know more about it.

7. Cut a strip of braiding a little larger than the circumference of the pot. Glue to the top edge of the pot with a glue gun. Fold the strips one by one towards the inside of the pot. Glue them with a glue gun. R with a glue gun.9. The pot is ready to accommodate the pencils in your office.

Birth Announcement Card

Make an announcement using different Parisian ties to celebrate the birth of your child.

Materials:

- An assortment of Parisian ties "newborn girl."

- An assortment of 80 Parisian ties. Pink.

- Alphabet Glitter uppercase. Pink.

- 25 Pollen folded cards 135x135 mm. White.

- Mahé sheet 30.5 x 30.5 cm. White.

- Mahé sheet 30.5 x 30.5 cm. Pale pink.
- Tube of universal gel glue 30 ml. Cultura.
- Self-healing cutting mat. 30x22 cm.
- An assortment of 3 precision tools.
- Template to download and print.

Steps:

1. To start, download, print, and reproduce the heart template. Hollow out the pattern using the cutter to create a stencil.
2. Cut an 11 x 11 cm pink square and a 10.5 x 10.5 cm white square.
3. Center the stencil on the square of white paper and secure it with adhesive paper to prevent it from moving.
4. Place a few Parisian ties to guide you in their positioning inside the cutout heart.
5. Using a precision cutter or paper punch, pierce your card and insert the Parisian clips.
6. Once the heart is filled, glue the white part on the rose.
7. Finish by pasting the desired text (first name.) to finalize the card.
8. The invitation is ready.

Cloud Shelf

Decorate this shelf cloud beautiful papers to Koala's reasons for decorating children's room very softly.

Materials:

- Créalia "Clouds" wooden shelf.
- Acrylic tube 120 matt white.
- Flat synthetic brush n° 18.
- Straight scissors 17 cm.
- Self-healing cutting mat 45x35 cm.

- Cardboard stickers. Little baby.
- Extra strong double-sided adhesive tape. 6mm x 10m.

Steps:

1. Paint the cloud shelf white. Let dry.
2. Download and transfer the templates to different papers from the collection and compose the decoration.
3. Glue the cut papers on the cloud shelf using the extra-strong double-sided tape.
4. Personalize the shelf with stickers from the collection.
5. Tip: the 30 x 30 cm block of paper offers visuals to frame to decorate your child's room or make scrapbooking albums.
6. The cloud shelf is ready to decorate your child's room.

DIY Bookmark Cat-page

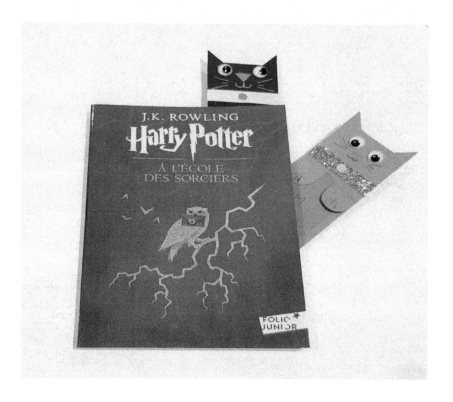

Materials:

- Block of 20 multi-colored cartoline sheets.
- Glue.
- Pouch of 24 decorated colored pencils.
- 6 round movable eyes Ø 12mm.
- Perfo round clamp 6mm.
- 5m roll of Glitter masking tape. Green.
- 5m roll of Glitter masking tape. White.

Steps:

1. Print the template and choose its paper colors.
2. Cut out the template along the lines.
3. Copy the drawing of the body, front legs, and back legs on the brown sheet, do the same in the purple sheet for the belly and cut out.
4. Glue the elements together with glue.
5. To facilitate the gluing, put a little glue on a cardboard plate and use a brush to spread the glue well. Then clean the brush with warm water and soap.
6. Glue the movable eyes, glue a piece of masking tape to make the collar, cut a piece of pink paper in a triangle for the nose, and draw the mouth, mustaches, and legs with a black pencil.
7. With the hole punch, make a small circle in the yellow paper and glue it to finalize the cat's collar.
8. To get an easy triangle nose, first cut out a square and cut it in half diagonally.
9. Write your name on the cat's belly with a colored pencil.
10. And there you have a nice cat-page bookmark for your summer readings. I'm going to reread the adventures of the little wizard, and what will you read?

You can even do it in other colors so that it doesn't get boring!

Table Decoration

Create a fresh and summery decoration for a tropical atmosphere, both on your walls and on your tables! Ideal for your summer evenings to share without moderation!

Materials:

- Set of 6 scrapbooking paper sheets. Tropical Paradise.
- Mahé Leaf—30.5x30.5cm. Petrol blue.
- Mahé Leaf—30.5x30.5cm. Menthol green.

28

- Mahé Leaf—30.5x30.5cm. Lime green.

- Mahé Leaf—30.5x30.5cm. Spring green.

- Slate scrapbooking sheet. Mahé 30x30cm.

- A sheet of 34 epoxy stickers. Tropical paradise.

- Eight card stock polaroid frames. Tropical paradise.

- An assortment of 40 die-cuts. Tropical paradise.

- 100m two-tone spool. Sky blue.

- 16 mini clothespins 35 mm.

- Vivaldi smooth sheet A4 240g. Canson white n° 1.

- Precision cutter and three blades.

- Blue cutting mat 2mm A3.

- Black acrylic and aluminum ruler 30cm.

- Precision scissors 13.5cm blue bi-material rings.

- 3D adhesive squares.

- Mahé Tools. Easy Mounter scrapbooking.

- Pack of 6 HB graphite pencils.

Steps:

1. Gather the materials.

2. Using the template and a pencil, reproduce the palm tree on the papers in the collection.

3. Download and print the template here.

4. Cut out with a cutter or scissors.

5. Assemble the trunk of the palm tree. Glue the foliage. Using the template, reproduce the traces of the cocktail support on thin cardboard, following the dimensions indicated. Cover it with the collection paper.

6. Download and print the template here.

7. After having cut in the slate sheet: 1 x (8.5 x 8.5 cm), choose a Polaroid. Glue the slate sheet to the back of the Polaroid. Using a chalk pen, write "Cocktail of the day." Decorate with the stickers. Fold the support at the dotted lines.

8. Using the templates and a pencil, draw the leaves and flowers on the Mahé paper and the collection paper. Draw.

9. Download and print the leaf and flower template.

10. Choose photos. Next, cut them to size: 8.5 x 8.5 cm. Stick to the back of the Polaroids.

11. Glue the leaves and flowers together. Cut the string to the desired dimensions and glue it to the back of the flowers. Glue the birds on the string and hang the photos using mini clips.

And here is a pretty summer and tropical decoration! Beautiful evenings in perspective!

Clothespin Card

Materials:

- Clothespin.
- Glue.
- Painting.
- Color paper or illustrations to download.
- Decorations: eyes, sequins.

Steps:

1. Start by painting your clothespins.

2. Cut out the illustrations or your colored paper in a heart shape.

3. Come and cut your shape in half in the middle.

4. Apply glue to the ends of your clothespin.

5. And stick your heart or your butterfly on your clothespin.

6. We now add glue to the back of your clothespin to be able to place the small text "I love you."

7. You can also add small decorations to customize your clothespin further. The card for your laundry is now ready to use.

Personalized Paper Bookmark

Materials:

- Cardstock 8 ½" by color and type of your choice.

- A green Standard Grip mat.

- Weeding tool.

- A Spatula.

- Pair of scissors.

Steps:

1. Begin a new project in the design space.

2. Choose shapes and select the square.

3. Unlock the square by clicking on the little lock at the bottom left-hand corner of the square.

4. With the square selected, change the shape to 6" wide.

5. With the square still selected, click on duplicate in the box on the right-hand side.

6. Select the copy you have made of the rectangle. Unlock it, and set the width to 5.5" by 0.5" height.

7. Move the smaller box into the middle of the larger box.

8. Select both of the shapes, and click on slice at the bottom-right-hand corner of the screen.

9. Remove the box in the middle of the rectangle and delete it.

10. In the middle of the larger box, you will see another smaller rectangular shape. Select it, move it out of the larger box, and delete it.

11. Select text from the left-hand menu. Choose a font. A good one for this is Bauhaus 9 or cooper black.

12. Type the name for the bookmark, "Chloe."

13. Move the name to the middle of the rectangle box, centering it, and then stretching it so it fills the hollow middle of the rectangle.

14. Select the rectangle and the name, click on copy, and make another three. You can make around four to five bookmarks on an 8 ½" by cardstock.

15. Change the names on the other three bookmarks. Highlight each one separately, and then clicks on weld in the bottom-right-hand corner (this must be done to each bookmark separately).

16. Save your project.

17. Place your cardstock onto the cutting mat, and load it into the Cricut.

18. Click Make it in the design space.

19. Select the materials, which will be the cardstock you have chosen.

20. Check that all the cartridges are loaded in the Cricut and that you have the fine-point blade loaded.

21. When the Cricut flashes ready, press go to cut out your cards.

22. When the printing is finished, remove the cardstock from the cutting mat, and use the spatula to ensure it comes off without ruining the cut.

23. Clean up the letters with the weeding tool.

24. Your bookmarks are ready for use.

Fancy Leather Bookmark

Materials:

- Cricut metallic leather.

- Cricut holographic iron-on—red for a gold effect.

- Purple strong-grip mat.

- Cricut fine-point blade.

- A weeding tool.

- Scissors for cutting the material to size.

- Brayer or scraping tool.

- Thin gold string or ribbon.

Steps:

1. Cut the leather to the size you want it to be.

2. Each leather holder is approximately 6" high.

3. Cut the holographic paper to the size you want it to be. This will depend on the size of the font and wording you choose for the bookmark.

4. Start a new project in the design space.

5. Select shapes from the left-hand menu.

6. Choose the square, unlock it, and set it with a height of 6."

7. Choose a triangle from the shapes menu, and set the width to 0.98" and the height to 0.9."

8. Position the triangle in the rectangle at the bottom. Make sure it is positioned evenly, as this is going to create a swallowtail for the bookmark.

9. Select the circle from the shapes menu and unlock the shape. Set the width and height to 0.8."

10. Duplicate the circle shape.

11. Move the one circle to the top-right-hand corner of the bookmark, and the other to the left. These will be the holes to put a piece of ribbon or fancy string through.

12. Align the holes and distribute them evenly, by using the align function from the top menu with both circles selected.

13. Select the top-left hole with the top of the rectangle, and click slice in the bottom-right menu.

14. Select the circle and remove it. Then delete it.

15. Select the top-right circle with the top of the rectangle, and click Slice from the bottom-right menu.

16. Select the circle and remove it.

17. Select the bookmark and move it over until you see the other two circles.

18. Select the two circles, and delete them.

19. Select the triangle and the bottom of the rectangle, then click Slice from the bottom-right-hand menu.

20. Select the first triangle; remove it, and delete it.

21. Select the second triangle; remove it, and delete it.

22. Save your project.

23. You will now have the first part of your leather bookmark ready to print.

24. Place the leather on the cutting mat, and use the brayer tool or scraper tool to flatten it and stick it properly to the cutting mat.

25. Position the little rollers on the feeding bar to the left and right, so they do not run over the leather.

26. Set the dial on the Cricut to custom.

27. Load the knife blade into the second Cricut chamber.

28. In the design space, click on make it.

29. Set the material to Cricut metallic leather.

30. Load the cutting board and leather into the Cricut, and click Go when the Cricut is ready to cut.

31. Unload the cutting board when the Cricut is finished printing, and use the spatula to cut the leather bookmark form out.

32. Use the weeding tool to remove any shapes that should not be on the bookmark.

33. Place the holographic paper on the cutting mat, and put the wheels on the loading bar back into their position.

34. Create a new project in the design space, and choose a nice, fancy font. Do not make it any bigger than 0.5" wide.

35. Save the project.

36. Click on make it, and choose the correct material.

37. Mirror the image.

38. Switch the blade in the second chamber back to the fine-point blade.

39. Load the cutting board, and click Go when the Cricut is ready to cut.

40. Gently peel the back off the design, heat the leather, and place the name on the bookmark where you want it positioned.

41. Use the same iron-on method as the method in the "Queen B" T-shirt project.

Your bookmark is now ready to use or give as a personalized gift.

Personalized Envelopes

Materials:

- Envelope 5.5" by .5".

- Cricut pens in the color of your choice.

- Standard grip mat.

- Spatula.

Steps:

1. Make a new project in the design space.

2. Choose the square from the shapes menu.

3. Unlock the square, set the width to 5.5" and the height to 0.5".

4. Choose text from the right-hand menu.

5. This will be the name and address the envelope will be addressed to.

6. Choose a font, and size it to fit comfortably in the middle of the envelope.

7. You can choose a different color for the font.

8. Move the text box to the middle of the envelope.

9. Select the entire envelope, and click attach from the bottom-right-hand menu.

10. When you move the card around the screen, the address text will move with the envelope.

11. Load the envelope onto the cutting board, and load it into the Cricut.

12. In design space, click Make it.

13. Choose the material like paper.

14. Check to see if the pen color you need is loaded into the first compartment of the Cricut.

15. When the project is ready, press Go and let it print.

16. Flip the card over, and stick it onto the mat.

17. Use a piece of tape to stick the envelope flap down.

18. Load it into the Cricut.

19. Change the text on the envelope to a "return address" or "regards from."

20. Change the color of the pen if you want the writing in another color.

21. When you are ready, click on Make it.

22. Make sure the material is set to the correct setting.

23. When you are ready, press Go.

24. Once it has finished cutting, you will have a personalized envelope.

Pumpkin Pillows

Materials:

- Burlap pad spread.

- Printable warmth moves.

- Material paper (whenever required for your image of move).

- Iron.

- Printer and ink.

- Pumpkin record of your decision.

Steps:

1. Download the pumpkin records that you might want to use to your PC as a jpg document. Utilize the Transfer button in the configuration space to import. For the blue pumpkin particularly, make certain to pick the unpredictable picture type. The other two imported fine with the reasonably unpredictable setting.

2. When you add it to the canvas, you can see that it is a print at that point cut by the layer's menu on the correct hand side.

3. Resize to whatever size that your requirement for your pumpkin pad. You should recall the size of your warm move. The Cricut will likewise print an outskirt around the picture so as to see it on the machine. It will provoke you to be that as it may if the picture is too huge even to consider fitting with the fringe.

4. Snap makes it and the product will incite you to print at that point cut your document. Ensure that the material size is right for your image of warmth move.

5. First, the product will permit you to print your picture. Make certain to utilize the best quality printing regardless of what brand of printer you are utilizing.

Burlaps

Materials:

- Burlap (a genuinely tight weave works best).
- Shabby glue.
- Pouncer brush.
- Wax paper.
- Cricut Maker (want to see the distinction between the machines? I thought about the Cricut Maker and Explore here.)

NOTE: my suggestion is to utilize the Maker for all texture ventures including this one.

- Cricut strong grip move tape.
- Cricut green tangle.
- Earthenware pot (the one I utilized was roughly 3 creeps in distance across at the top).
- Styrofoam ball.
- Greenery.
- Craft glue and paste firearm.
- Cricut delicious document.

Steps:

1. Start with a 12 x 12 square of burlap and lay it on certain was paper to ensure your work surface. Blend tasteless paste creamer in with water. At that point utilize a pouncer brush to apply this blend all over your burlap.

2. Permit to dry. This will take in any event for the time being. At that point simply strip your hardened burlap from the wax paper sheet. Presently we need to get this solid material to adhere to a Cricut tangle. Apply solid grasp move tape to the rear of your burlap. At that point place the non-clingy side of your exchange tape down onto your tangle. Press it down truly well. You can even utilize a brayer or moving pin here.

3. Access the delicious cut record in configuration space by clicking here. At that point resize with the goal that your littlest piece isn't under 1 3/4 inches.

Felt Banners

Materials:

- Dowel the slice to 5.5.

- Felt.

- Heated glue.

- Yarn.

Steps:

1. Plug in your heated glue firearm to get it warmed up, at that point cut your felt utilizing the turning sharp edge and texture tangle. Strip away the additional felt. It resembles enchantment!

2. Strip off the flag. Spot the dowel on top, and crease over the top edge to see where the dowel should be set.

3. Include a line of craft glue.

4. Carefully overlay the top over. On the off chance that you have a low-temp stick firearm or thick felt, you may have the option to squeeze it down with your fingers... yet to be protected you could utilize a pencil or the rest of the dowel so you don't consume your fingers.

5-Coffee Sleeves

Espresso sleeves make an extremely extraordinary and cheap blessing thought.

Materials:

- Felt (I utilized the Cricut felt sheets).
- Iron-on vinyl (I utilized the sparkle vinyl in silver).
- Cricut cutting machine.
- Weeding instruments (discretionary).
- Cricut easy-press (discretionary however suggested—see underneath for subtleties).
- Velcro.

- Texture paste or sewing machine.

- Cut document.

Steps:

1. Start by cutting your pieces. Cut the words from sparkle iron-on vinyl utilizing your fine point cutting edge. Make sure to reflect the cuts on the iron-on vinyl and spot it glossy side down on your tangle. Cut the sleeve itself from felt. On the off chance that your territory cutting two of the sleeves one after another, you might need to change the situation inside the design space to capitalize on your material. It needs to cut every sleeve from one sheet of felt.

2. Start by featuring your first tangle with a sleeve. At that point click on the sleeve itself.

3. Next, snap the second tangle that has a sleeve. Snap the sleeve itself and snap the three dabs. At that point pick "move to another tangle."

4. Pick the tangle with the principal sleeve.

5. Presently you simply need to turn it and move the position so it isn't covering the first. You would now be able to cut two sleeves from one sheet of felt.

6. Expel all overabundance from your vinyl pattern including the focuses of your letters.

How to Cut Bass Wood with Your Cricut Maker Machine?

Materials:

- Cricut machine (Maker or Expression).
- 3"x24" bass wood.
- Rotary blade.
- Painter's tape.

Steps:

1. Before you unload your material from the machine, ensure that you check your project and that the cut was done all the way. If the cut is not all the way, you can restart the cut all over again as long as you did not eject or move the mat.
2. The design space will also be notifying you of the progress of the cut: how many passes to complete your project, and the amount of time remaining to finish your project. This is amazing as it will help you get the progress of your work any time you check on it. That is, in case, you need to carry out other pressing tasks at hand. You have the design in your Cricut design space already, so click Continue.

3. Select the type of material by clicking on Browse all materials. Type in bass wood in the materials and choose the type of bass wood, preferably 1/16 basswood.

4. Click Done. Ensure that you follow the instructions on the cutting window by moving the star wheel (white in color) to the right of the machine. I believe that you still remember why this is important. Then, the materials should be secured to the strong grip mat using tape. Of course, the material should not be more than 11" wide.

5. Insert the rotary blade into the accessory clamp. By the way, the machine will give a warning if the blade is not inserted. Now, you load the mat into the machine by pressing the Load/unload button.

6. The machine will start cutting when you press the flashing Cricut button. It will make an entire pass of the image the machine is going to cut before cutting the full image. Of course, this will take time because of the thickness of the cut.

7. Unload the mat by pressing the Load/unload button which will be blinking when the task is completed.

8. Remove the tape and your material from the mat.

9. Use the weeding tool to remove your design from the whole material gently.

How to Do Cake Toppers Using Your Cricut Maker

Materials:

- Cricut Maker machine.
- Cricut spatula.
- Lightweight chipboard.
- Cake sticks.

Steps:

1. Open a new project in your Cricut design space, click on text tool and type in your desired text. Change the text to your favorite font.
2. Ungroup the letters and arrange them to be slightly overlapping as shown below. Do these, word by word, in case you have more than one word.
3. Weld the word together separately.

NOTE: What if you have the letter "I" in your expression, how do you connect the floating dot? It is very simple. All you need to do is:

4. Go to shapes and select Cycle.

5. Resize the size of the cycle to be slightly bigger than the floating dot.

6. Move the cycle over the floating dot.

7. Select the whole word where the letter "I" is contained and then select Slice. The essence of this is to separate the floating dot from the letter "I."

8. Move the cycle back to join the letter "I" without the floating dot and weld it together.

9. When you have done this for all the letters "I," join the words together by touching each other in as many places as possible. This will make the cake topper to be as stable as possible.

10. Weld them all together.

11. Resize it to taste by increasing or decreasing the dimensions.

12. Now is time to make it. Send it to the mat. Set the dial to Customs and select Lightweight chipboard.

13. Place your lightweight chipboard on the mat and load it into the machine by pressing Load/unload button. Press the flashing Cricut button.

14. Use a Cricut spatula to remove the cake topper from the mat when the job is done and after unloading the mat from the machine. You remember how to unload, right? Yes, you do.

15. Remove the unwanted and extra chipboard from your design.

16. Finally, attach your cake stick to the middle of your design with the aid of glue. If you have a long-expression, use two or more sticks depending on the size of your cake.

CHAPTER 2

FAQ, TIPS, AND TRICKS

Although we have answered most of the questions that might come up when you start using your shiny, new Cricut machine, here are some questions that beginners usually have. With these answers, you won't have any trouble when using your Cricut machine, and you can start running wild with your creativity!

Can Cricut Design Space Work on More Than One Mobile Device or Computer?

Yes, it can! Cricut design space, as mentioned earlier, is cloud-based. No matter where you are or the kind of device that you are using, you can always use this application as long as it is compatible. If you're logged in at home, you can also log in on your phone if you're on the go.

Do I Have to Have an Internet Connection Before I Use Cricut Design Space?

Using Cricut design space on a laptop or a computer requires a high-speed internet connection. The internet must be high-speed broadband if you want your design to go smoothly. iOS users can get the app's offline version if they have the latest version of the design space.

How Do I Find the Cricut Access Fonts and Images on Design Space?

With their new update, everything that is available on Cricut access has a green "a" marking. This means that while you explore images and fonts, you can easily distinguish which one is from Cricut access and which isn't. When searching for something, use filters too to narrow your search.

Is It Possible to Disable the Grid on the Canvas Area?

Yes, you can! If you're not comfortable or you don't want to use the gridlines, you can toggle them in your settings. To do this, you open your account menu and click on settings. Click on canvas grid, and from there, you can turn the gridlines off.

For those using an iOS device, settings have been provided for you at the bottom of the screen. With them, you can turn the grid line on and off.

Do I Need to Pay to Use Design Space?

No, you don't. Design space comes completely free. You only need a subscription if you plan on using Cricut access. But, if you need the basics, then you can open a design space account for free.

What Is the Cricut Tote Bag?

If you plan to travel with your Cricut machine and supplies or need somewhere to store them when you're not using them, you can purchase a Cricut tote bag.

The Cricut machine tote bag is for all the cutting machines. It can fit anyone you own. The Cricut rolling craft tote bag is for supplies only, and the cutting machine can't fit in it. The kits come in purple, navy, and raspberry.

There is also the tweed Cricut tote bag, an older version of the new tote bags.

Will My New Cricut Explore Machine Come with a Carry Bag?

Sadly, it won't. This doesn't mean that you cannot buy a carry bag or machine tote back from Cricut separately.

Will a Cricut Maker Fit into the Tweed Machine Tote?

Yes, it will. If you need somewhere to place your Cricut maker for convenience, you can easily purchase a machine tote from Cricut.

Do I Have to Buy a Wireless Bluetooth Adapter When I Buy an Explore Machine?

If you bought the Explore Air and Explore Air 2, you don't have to buy a wireless Bluetooth adapter. But this is not the same for the Explore One, and so you can buy the Cricut wireless Bluetooth adapter if that's what you wish.

The Cricut Maker Can Know the Blade I Loaded Without a Smart Dial. How?

The machine moves the carriage to the right before cutting your project. This is called homing. Here, the device will scan the blade and know which one you installed.

If I Upgrade from an Explore to a Cricut Maker, Will I Lose My Projects and Cartridges?

No, you won't. All your information is not linked to the Cricut machine. Instead, it is connected to your Cricut ID in the Cricut cloud. As long as you're using the same ID, you will have access to all your information and projects when you get a new Cricut machine.

Does My Cricut Machine Have to Be Connected to the Internet?

Your Cricut machine does not work alone, but instead, it has to be connected to the design space. The design space uses an internet connection, except you're using the offline version on your iOS device.

Do I Use the Same Design Space for Both the Explore Series and Cricut Maker?

Your design space will not change even if you are switching from one Cricut machine to another. Also, no matter which one you're using, you always have to use design space. But, Cricut Maker has more design space benefits than the explore series.

CHAPTER 3

FAQS AND TIPS TO KEEP CRICUT MAKER EFFICIENT

Where Can I Use Cricut Design Space?

You can use Cricut design space through your web browser on PC or Mac after downloading the plugin. You can also download the app on your tablet or smartphone on iOS or Android.

What Is Cricut Access?

This is Cricut's subscription service to their library of images and fonts in the Cricut design space. It gives access to more than 30,000 images, 370 fonts, and premium project ideas, as well as 10% off all purchases on the Cricut website. There are different types of plans available, ranging from $4.99 to $9.99 per month.

How Do I Install Design Space?

Design space will give you a prompt to download and install the plugin. Click Download and wait for it to finish. Once it does, click the file to install the plugin. You might get a box asking for permission; if so, allow it. Follow the prompts through the installer. You're now ready to use design space!

Why Am I Getting Error Messages about the Design Space Plugin?

If you're getting error messages or having difficulty using design space, you may need to reinstall the plugin. Expand your computer's system tray on the lower right-hand side of the screen and locate the Cricut icon. Right-click on it and click Exit. Open your web browser and navigate to design.Cricut.com and sign in with your Cricut ID. Once prompted, download and install the plugin again.

Do I Need a Computer to Use My Cricut Machine?

No! If you have the Cricut Explore Air or the Cricut Maker, you can utilize the built-in Bluetooth to connect to your mobile device and download the design space app on it.

What's the Difference Between the Cricut Explore One and the Cricut Explore Air 2?

The Cricut Explore One has a single tool carriage, so if you do more than one action (cut and write or cut and score), it will need to do it in two steps, and you'll need to switch out the tools between them. The Cricut Explore Air 2 has two tool carriages, so it can do both functions in one step with no need to switch tools. Explore Air 2 also has built-in Bluetooth connectivity.

Do I Use the Same Cricut Design Space for the Cricut Maker?

Yes! The only difference is that you'll have the option to adjust the material settings in the design space since the Maker does not have the dial on the machine itself.

How Does the Cricut Maker Know Which Blade Is in the Carriage?

The machine scans the blade before it cuts a project.

What Is the Thickness of a Material That the Cricut Maker Can Cut?

3/32" of an inch or 2.4mm when using the rotary blade or the knife blade.

How Do I Get a Good Transfer Using the Cricut Easy Press?

Use the easy press on a firm and even surface. Check the iron-on material and the base material for the recommended settings and use those. Be sure to apply heat to both the front and back of the project for the recommended amount of time.

How Much Pressure Does the Cricut Easy Press Need?

Check the recommendations for the material you're using. Some will call for "firm" pressure, meaning you should use two hands and about 15–20 lbs. of body weight. Others need "gentle" pressure, meaning you should use one hand with about 5–10 lbs. of body weight. Use your easy press on a waist-high table for the easiest way to apply pressure.

Do I Move the Cricut Easy Press Around like an Iron?

Keep the easy press in one spot for the recommended amount of time. Moving it might smear or warp the design.

Why Should I Use the Cricut Easy Press?

It heats more evenly and more quickly than iron and is easy to use. It will give you more professional-looking iron-owns and takes 60 seconds or less.

How Do I Protect Surfaces While Using the Cricut Easy Press?

Cricut recommends using the Cricut easy press mat, which comes in three different sizes. However, you can also use a cotton bath towel with an even texture folded to about 3 inches thick. Do not use an ironing board, as the surface isn't even enough, and it's too unsteady to apply appropriate pressure. Silicone baking mats and aluminum foil don't provide enough insulation and can get dangerously hot.

My Material Is Tearing! Why?

The most common reason is that your mat isn't sticky enough. It could have lost its stickiness, or you aren't using the right mat for the material. It could also be that the blade needs to be replaced or sharpened, or you're using the wrong type of blade. Materials can also tear if the machine is in the wrong setting.

Why Won't My Transfer Tape Work?

More often than not, it's not working when you try to use standard transfer tape with glitter vinyl. It requires the Cricut strong grip transfer tape. It's too strong to use with regular vinyl, though, so keep using the regular transfer tape for that.

What Type of Mat Should I Use?

Each mat has a specific use. Here's each one and some suggestions of what material to use with them.

Blue

- **Light grip mat:** thinner paper, vellum, construction paper, sticky notes, light vinyl, and wrapping paper.

Green

- **Standard grip mat:** cardstock, thicker paper, washi paper, vinyl, and bonded fabric.

Purple

- **Strong grip mat:** thick cardstock, magnet sheets, chipboard, poster board, fabric with stiffener, aluminum foil, foam, leather, and suede.

Pink

- **Fabric grip mat:** fabric, bonded fabric, and crepe paper.

How Do I Wash My Mats?

Place the mat in the sink, supported by a firm flat surface. Running lukewarm water over it, use a hard-bristled brush to scrub it gently in circles until the mat is clean. Pat dry with a paper towel and let it air dry for the stickiness to return.

Why Won't My Blade Cut All the Way Through the Material?

Make sure that the blade is completely in the carriage, and make sure there's no debris around it. Check that your settings are for the correct material. If you're still having trouble, slowly increase the pressure and do test cuts until it gets all the way through.

Can I Upload My Own Images to the Cricut Design Space?

Yes! It's easy to upload your own image and create a design with it. On the left side of the design space, there is an option for "upload Images."

What Is Infusible Ink?

Infusible ink is a new system from Cricut that infuses ink directly into compatible Cricut blanks. There are infusible ink transfer sheets and infusible ink pens and markers. They are applied using heat, such as with the Cricut easy press.

Does Cricut Design Space Require an Internet Connection?

Yes.

What Weight Is Cricut Cardstock?

80 lb.

What Are the Care Instructions for Cricut Iron-On Material?

Wash and dry the item inside out in a delicate style. If you notice areas of the iron-on material coming off after being washed, iron it again, following the full application instructions.

What's a Quick Reference List of Materials I Can Cut?

For the Explore machines: all paper, all cardstock, vinyl, bonded fabrics, corrugated paper, sticker paper, and parchment paper. For the Maker machine: all of the above, plus fabric and textiles and thin wood.

Do I Have to Use Cricut Brand Materials?

No! You can use any brand of materials that you want. Thickness and quality are the only things that matter.

What Pens Can I Use in My Cricut Machine?

The Cricut brand pens will, of course, fit into your machine. However, some others will fit in the pen holder as well. Some users have found ways to adapt other pens, but the pens and markers in the following list don't require any adjustments.

- Wal-Mart leisure arts markers.
- Target dual-tip markers.
- Pilot precise V5 pens.
- Thin Crayola markers.
- Dollar tree jot markers.
- Bic round stic pen.

What Is the Cricut Adaptive Tool System?

This is a new feature in the Cricut Maker. It adjusts the direction and pressure of the blades throughout the cutting process. It allows for much more precise cuts and much higher cutting pressure.

What Is the Scoring Wheel?

A scoring wheel is a tool for the Cricut Maker, as it uses the adaptive tool system. It creates fold lines in thicker materials. The scoring stylus also makes fold lines.

How Small Can the Rotary Blade Cut?

Cricut recommends keeping designs above ¾". Any smaller than that, the blade might gouge into your mat as it turns, damaging the mat and dulling the blade.

What Is the Fast Mode?

This is a feature on the Cricut Explore Air 2 and Cricut Maker. It allows you to cut and write twice as fast when the machine is set to vinyl, iron-on, or cardstock.

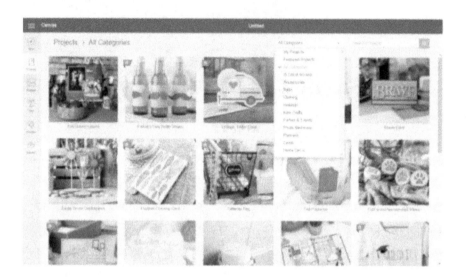

Do I Have to Have an Internet Connection Before I Use Cricut Design Space?

Using Cricut design space on a laptop or a computer requires a high-speed internet connection. The internet must be high-speed broadband if you want your design to go smoothly. iOS users can get the offline version of the app if they have the latest version of the design space.

Is There a Difference Between Digital and Physical Cartridges?

A cartridge, in the Cricut sense, generally refers to image sets. So, a cartridge is made up of images that have the same theme. Cartridges can be either digital or physical, although a lot of the physical cartridges have been retired. You can purchase the digital cartridges on Cricut.com.

How Do I Find the Cricut Access Fonts and Images on Design Space?

With their new update, everything that is available on Cricut access has a green "a" marking. This means that while you explore images and fonts, you can easily distinguish which one is from Cricut access and which isn't. When searching for something, use filters too to narrow your search.

How Long Do I Own the Images That I Purchase in Design Space?

Cricut images don't expire! That's right. Once you pay for them, you own them, and they remain in your library until you don't need them anymore.

Is It Possible to Disable the Grid on the Canvas Area?

Yes, you can! If you're not comfortable or you don't want to use the gridlines, you can toggle them in your settings. To do this, you open your account menu and click on settings. Click on Canvas grid and from there, you can turn the grid lines off.

For those using an iOS device, settings have been provided for you at the bottom of the screen. With them, you can turn the grid line on and off.

Is Design Space Compatible with a Chromebook Computer?

No, it isn't. The latest version of the Cricut design space only works with Windows or a Mac operating system.

Do I Need to Pay in Order to Use Design Space?

No, you don't. Design space comes completely free. You only need a subscription if you plan on using Cricut access. But, if you need the basics, then you can open a design space account for free.

CHAPTER 4

BUSINESS IDEAS:
INTRODUCTION

The Benefits of Creating a Business and Selling What You Create

Making money with your crafts is not as hard as you might think. First, decide whether you want to start a small business or you want your hobby to pay for itself.

You can run a craft business from your own home without investing in office or retail space. You choose your hours and the types of projects you want to produce. It's a chance to use your creativity and also make extra money.

Things to Consider Before Starting Your Craft Business

There are always legalities to consider when starting any business. They change from state to state and even from city to city. So, you'll need to check online for your local laws. You may need to obtain a local license or file for a fictitious name certificate. This shows you're doing business as (DBA) Sally's Crafts or Alice's Craft Emporium.

In the beginning, you can probably work as a sole proprietor and won't need to incorporate. You'll file a schedule C with your tax return.

You'll need to track your income and expenses carefully. You will be responsible for paying taxes on the money you earn. But you only need to pay tax on the profits. You can subtract the money you spend on materials and equipment.

Remember: self-employment tax is higher than the tax rate you pay as an employee. Put money aside so you'll have it when taxes are due. You may need to set up quarterly tax payments to avoid penalties. Talking to an accountant is always a good idea since the tax laws change.

To start with, you may want to track your income and expenses on a spreadsheet. But when possible invest in software such as quicken. This will make your job much more comfortable; plus, you can print out reports to take to your accountant once a year. This will decrease his fees since he'll have less work to do.

Starting a sideline business can be time-consuming. It's best if you can get your family on board from the beginning. Let them know how the extra money will take the stress off the family budget or maybe help pay for an unforgettable vacation. If your family knows what you're working towards, they'll be more excited about helping you. Teenagers may be able to work in the business with you and learn valuable skills.

Building a Brand; Building an Audience

One reason why Etsy is so popular is they pride themselves on bringing artists and customers together to develop a relationship. So, it's your job to tell people who you are and why they should buy from you.

To build your credibility post videos on YouTube that explain the process you use to create crafts. This helps brand you as an expert. Plus, even though viewers might like to learn to do the projects themselves; they often decide it's not worth the time and effort and will click through to purchase from your website.

Always link back to your main website or craft store from your social media sites. Set up your signature to include your business contact information when posting to online forums and in your email.

Keep your business name in front of your customers, and make it easy for them to find you. Include a business card or refrigerator magnet with your company info on it with every new order. Include an extra business card and ask them to hand it to a friend.

The customer is always right.

Always offer excellent customer service. If someone emails you with a question, get back to them as soon as possible. Package and ship your products carefully. Make sure you add enough to your shipping costs to allow for postage and packaging. You may want to offer gift wrapping for an extra charge.

Ask for feedback. It's the best way to find out how to improve your service. Make it easy for customers to leave testimonials on your web page. A happy customer goes a long way in building your credibility. State your return or refund policy clearly on your website, so there are no surprises for your customers.

Creating projects with your Circuit, can be more than just a fun hobby. If you're willing to put in the effort, you can build a sideline or even a full-time business while doing something you love.

Logo, Licenses, Copyright

Since you decided to get into this business, we should talk about the legalities of starting a craft business. There are many rules about licenses and copyrights and it is important to understand them so the inception of your business won't be affected. Copyright is especially a big issue because often we use templates, pictures, produced or created by others on the internet. It doesn't mean that just because it is on the internet that we are free to use and we can a profit from it. Different multimedia or pictures have different copyright the most common that you have to be familiar with in order to run a craft business successfully is the Cricut angel policy.

Cricut Angel Policy

The Cricut design space system comes with a set of images that may be used as a template and altered if you're just beginning with Cricut design. However, all these set of images that come with the software is protected under the "Cricut angel policy." This means we cannot use it to the extent that we wish. There are some limitations and guidelines that must be followed.

These are:

- Almost all images found in Cricut access are included under the Cricut angel policy.
- You're allowed only to create 10,000 images to be sold using Cricut images.
- You are not allowed to sell individual images.
- You are required to include a copyright notice with every project you make.
- You cannot include licensed content in your images, such as those by Disney and Marvel.

Personal Use vs. Commercial Use

Learn the basics so you can create something from scratch. But if you must really use pictures from Cricut, try to look for similar ones and buy them in online stores. Refrain from downloading pictures readily available on Google. Most of these pictures are under copyright and if you do you will be violating copyrights measure.

When purchasing any image online, make sure to read and understand the conditions and terms of use. Most of these purchases have an agreement that the picture can only use personally. This means the image cannot be used to be sold for business. It is only open for personal use. Some of the images contain an option to buy including a commercial license. Just be wary of the terminologies.

Some of the images that have strict copyright are from companies such as Disney and/or Marvel. Every character such as Elsa from Frozen, Doctor Strange from Marvel, Captain America, Thanos, and Iron Man are produced by these companies. If you use these images for your business and make a profit from it, you'll be breaking the copyright and you may be sued.

CHAPTER 5

WHERE I SHOULD SELL
MY PROJECTS

It is a well-known fact in the world of business that to make money, you first need to invest money. With that being said, if you already own a "Cricut" cutting machine, then you can jump to the next paragraph, but if you are debating if it's worth the investment, then read on.

As mentioned earlier, "Cricut" has a range of cutting machines with distinctive capabilities offered at a varying price range. The "Cricut Explore Air 2" is priced at $249.99, and the "Cricut Maker" is priced at $399.99 (the older "Cricut Explore Air" model may be available for sale on Amazon at a cheaper price). Now, if you were to buy any of these machines during a holiday sale with a bundle deal that comes with a variety of tools, accessories, and materials for a practice project as well as free trial membership to "Cricut Access," you would already be saving enough to justify the purchase for your personal usage.

The cherry on top would be if you can use this investment to make more money. You can always get additional supplies in a bundle deal or from your local stores at a much cheaper price. All in all, those upfront costs can easily be justified with the expenses you budget for school projects that require you to cut letters and shapes, create personalized gifts for your loved ones, or decorate your home with customized decals, and of course, your own jewelry creations.

These are only a handful of the reasons to buy a "Cricut" machine for your personal use. Let's start scraping the mountain of "Cricut" created wealth to help you get rich while enjoying your work!

At this stage, let's assume that you have bought a "Cricut" cutting machine and have enough practice with the beginner-friendly projects described earlier in this book. You now have the skillset and the tools to start making money with your "Cricut" machine, so let's jump into how you can make it happen. The ways listed below have been tried and tested as successful money-making strategies that you can implement with no hesitations.

Local Market

If you like the thrill of a show-and-tell, then reserve a booth at a local farmer's market and show up with some ready-to-sell crafts. In this case, you are relying on the number of people attending and a subset of those who might be interested in making a purchase from you. If you are in an urban neighborhood where people are keenly interested in unique art designs but do not have the time to create them on their own, you can easily make big bucks by setting a decent price point for your products.

Bring flyers to hand out people so they can reach you through one of your social media accounts or email and check all your existing Etsy listings. Think of these events as a means of marketing for those who are not as active online but can be excited with customized products to meet their next big life event like a baby shower, birthday party, or wedding.

One downside to participating in local events is the generation of mass inventory and booth displays, topped with expenses to load and transport the inventory. You may or may not be able to sell all of the inventory depending on the size of the event, but as I said earlier, you can still make the most of this by marketing your products and building up a local clientele.

Online: Social Media

We are all aware of how social media has become a marketing platform for not only established corporations, but also small businesses and budding entrepreneurs. Simply add hashtags like for sale, product, selling, free shipping, the sample included, and more to entice potential buyers. Join Facebook community pages and groups for handcraft sellers and buyers to market your products. Use catchy phrases like customization available at no extra cost or free returns if not satisfied when posting the products on these pages as well as your personal Facebook page. Use Twitter to share feedback from your satisfied customers to widen your customer base. You can do this by creating a satisfaction survey that you can email to your buyers or include a link to your Etsy listing asking for online reviews and ratings from your customers.

Another tip here is to post pictures of anything and everything you have created using "Cricut" machines, even those that you did not plan to sell. You never know who else might need something that you deemed unsellable.

Since you will be creating these only after the order has been placed, you can easily gather the required supplies after the fact and get crafting.

Etsy

Yes! Don't forget to check out the angel policy. You can sell items utilizing non-licensed images in the Cricut library, or you could design your graphics using illustrator or photoshop. You can't sell accredited pictures—Disney, Marvel Comics, etc. These pictures are very popular and you'll see Etsy stores selling these kinds of pictures, but these stores can be closed down or perhaps sued for selling accredited pictures.

Would You Market Cricut Layouts?

Yes! The Cricut angel policy permits you to sell around 10,000 layouts annually with discounts created with Provo craft solutions. There's room for one to increase your company, and sell layouts made using Cricut products. Just be certain that you read over the total angel policy to make certain you are working inside.

What Are the Most Lucrative Cricut Companies?

The most rewarding Cricut companies are people who provide unique products that people wish to purchase. Why waste your time creating products that nobody is considering? Rather spend your time exploring your competitors. Learn what other crafting organizations are doing well, and where they're making errors. This could enable you to locate a complete in your marketplace so you can create things with lesser competition.

Selling Finished Pieces

You would be using your "Cricut" machines for a variety of personal projects like home décor, holiday décor, personalized clothing, and more. Next time you embark on another one of your creative journeys leading to unique creations, just make two of everything, and you can easily put the other product to sell on your Etsy shop. Another great advantage is that you will be able to save all your projects on the design space application for future use, so if one of your projects goes viral, you can easily buy the supplies and turn them into money-making offerings. This way, not only your original idea for personal usage will be paid off, but you can make much more money than you invested in it, to begin with.

Again, spend some time researching what kind of designs and decorations are trending in the market and use them to spark up inspiration for your next project. Some of the current market trends include customized cake and cupcake toppers and watercolor designs that can be framed as fancy wall decorations. The cake toppers can be made with cardstock, which is another beginner-friendly material, light in weight, and can be economically shipped tucked inside an envelope.

Personalized Clothing and Accessories

T-shirts with cool designs and phrases are all the rage right now. Just follow a similar approach to the selling vinyl section and take it up a notch.

You can create sample clothing with an iron-on design and market it with "can be customized further at no extra charge" or "transfer the design on your own clothing" to get traction in the market.

You can buy sling bags and customize them with unique designs to be sold as finished products at a higher price than a plain boring sling bag.

Consider creating a line of products with a centralized theme like the DC Marvel characters or the Harry Potter movies and design custom t-shirts, hats, and even bodysuits for babies. You can create customized party favor boxes and gift bags at the request of the customer. Once your product has a dedicated customer base, you can get project ideas from them directly and quote them a price for your work. Isn't that great?

Another big advantage of the heat transfer vinyl, as mentioned earlier, is that anyone can transfer the design on their desired item of clothing using a standard household iron. But you would need to include the transfer instructions with the order, letting them know exactly how to prep for the heat transfer without damaging their chosen clothing item. And again, heat transfer vinyl can be easily shipped using a standard mailing envelope. We have added a dedicated section on tips for using everyday iron-on with a household iron.

CHAPTER 6

HOW TO SET MY PRICES?

It bothers me to see people selling their beautiful super elaborate creations at SO cheap prices. Those people aren't even valuing their own time. They are not taking under consideration your talent, materials, or many other things that are important when setting prices.

Monetizing Your Art

You have practiced, perfected, and established a method of that art that you like to do so much. You have got decorated cards, personalized objects, created pictures with motivational phrases, and proudly you have shared your work on social networks.

Now comes the question that scares you so much. "What would you charge to do this?" it is super exciting and flattering to understand that there are people that ask you to do what you love to earn money.

However, as exciting as it is, it scares us, and a lot. To be honest, I still feel nervous when sending a quote to my clients. We have all been there on several occasions, and I realize it is difficult initially, but the most important thing is to have everything in order.

Before you begin brooding about monetizing your art, you ought to think about all the factors that you might not have considered when valuing your work. Believe it or not, there are more reasons behind the costs, aside from "because that's what so-and-so charges." Alright, then let's start.

Someone Wants to Hire Me. What Do I Do Now?

Congratulations! You must be super excited, but before responding with a price, or worse, offering to do it for free of charge, there is a lot to think about when evaluating your work, and I hope I'm covering a large part here.

Why is pricing so important? Shouldn't I feel good just by putting the worth that I understand "correct"? Well, it is not wrong to ask yourself this question; however, you want to make sure that you aren't bothering yourself, the client, and other artists in the business.

When you are self-employed, you are responsible for the cash you earn, so you need to do it right. It is important that you ask yourself these questions before setting a price.

How much are your time and energy worth to you? How does your experience compare to others in the business? What are your material costs? What is the size of the project? What is the project deadline? Are you going to include shipping, or charge extra? Is this piece getting to be original, or is the customer making and selling multiple copies? Does the client want you to convert the artwork into a digital format? Will you be creating the artwork in your own studio or on-site? What will be your minimum charge for little jobs?

Your Time + Energy

This is where the wellness factor comes in, where you need to think about how much your time is worth to you. It's worth a lot more than buying the most cost-effective combo at McDonald's, but there the questions come... Karissa, how much exactly? How do I find out? It is difficult to answer this frankly but there are certain guidelines I can tell you that will help you.

The typical answer is that you put yourself a monthly salary with which you feel comfortable, I will speak in an imaginary way based on some local statistics of the Dominican Republic to speak with numbers and you can understand. For instance, (I made it up) on average a monthly salary in my country is $ 15,000 Dominican pesos and this is often the amount with which you value your time and energy.

This number is going to be divided by 4.3, this number is established as the average of weeks in the year since there are months that have 30 days, another 31, and February with 28. Already beginning to see the difference? Now try to use that math to calculate your own hourly rate.

Start with the monthly salary you feel comfortable with: _____.

Divide that number by 4.3 and put it here: _____.

Now divide this other number by 44 (remember that this number may change). So, this result's your hourly rate that you will put here: _____.

Your Level of Experience

You may have been practicing or creating for every week or a year before being asked about working for money. This is often more about the standard of your work, instead of how long you have been at it. But be careful: it is not that you are going to compare with artists who have a level of professionalism for a long time, it is a matter of an objective perspective. Is it clean? Is it consistent? Do you have your own style? Do you feel confident in your work? Have you ever taken workshops or courses to make sure your techniques are correct?

Cost of Materials

Are you using cheap store markers or artist-quality paints? Do you use expensive papers and ready inks? Are they special items you need? Do you need to order online that are specific to some part of the world or available near you?

The value increases with the standard of your tools and materials, also as your knowledge of them. If you answer "What type of paint do you have/ use?" With an "I do not know ... I've had it for a long time and the label it is no longer visible" or "a friend gave it to me, and I do not know where he got it," Your work won't be as valuable as that of somebody whose answer is "I exploit Winsor and Newton's lightweight, water-resistant watercolors." Artist-quality materials cost more, so it is vital that you know the value of your materials just in case they run out.

Also, for an enormous job, you will need to burn seven special markers. That is a part of the value that you don't want out of your time or pocket but is an expense that has to be included in your estimate.

Of course, if during a job you used only a part of the material, obviously, you are not going to charge the complete cost of that material, there you want to use mathematics, knowing beforehand how much of the fabric you used and getting a percentage.

Project Size

This is probably one of the primary factors to value your project. How big is it? Creating something, for instance, a lettering composition is an 8 ½ x 11-inch sheet with ten words will take much less time and lesser materials than those self-same ten words on an 8x10 footboard. You will have a price for measurements, for instance, square inches, or better use your hourly rate that we work above.

Delivery/Shipping Costs

You must indicate in your budget if the delivery is included or is an unprecedented payment. Meaning you need to understand where the piece goes. You will need to purchase parcel shipping quotes outside of your city based on the load size and repair you actually need. I like to recommend that you investigate the rates of the shipping companies and thus have a typical shipping cost.

Original or Continuous Use?

Will your client use your art once (like a marriage card), continuously (like a card or blog), or multiple times (like a T-shirt to resell)? It is always a good idea to ask this question beforehand. The answer will help you determine how valuable your artwork is to the customer if it will be used continuously to market or generate direct income for your client, the worth increases.

Deliverables

What do you have to deliver to your customer as a finished product? An ingenious art? Or is it digital? Both of them? What file formats? JPG, PNG, TIF, EPS, AI? Do you have experience digitizing, and do you have the best tools to do it?

Spending time digitizing and preparing multiple files takes time and knowledge, and thus should be priced accordingly. There also are those printed from digital art. Will you mail the file? In a memory? Digital start when you delivered it printed? All this must be taken under consideration, considering the time and energy it took to do it.

NOTE: a digital job is even costlier since it is often reproduced, and using specialized programs requires previous experience and learning, which I suppose also costs you to accumulate.

Location (In or Out of Your Studio)

Your hourly rate also will largely depend upon where you will be doing the work.

When you have the posh of your own space, you can perform several tasks at the same time; that means you can be working on two projects at the same time. This makes it easy to access all of your supplies and materials. The most convenient way for you to work is in your place, at your own pace with everything you need at hand, you ought to not worry about traffic.

If the work requires you to be somewhere outside your study (let's say a restaurant, for example), the worth of your time will increase significantly. You will have to go to and from the place (which must be included in your work time), carry all of your materials with you, and only plan to work during the assigned hours. That also means you will be in an uncontrolled environment, including distractions, noise, and curious people.

It is often a lot of fun working on site, and it is often a true headache. Sometimes, a mixture of your time in your studio and on-site works best. You can perform all the designs and preparatory add the studio to perform your duties once you arrive on site. This can be shown as two separate hourly rates in the quote, breaking down your activities, so your client knows how they are investing their money in you.

Project Term

Only you know what time is most comfortable for you to work. If not, I like to recommend measuring the time you are taking doing all of your work to have an estimate and an area just if something unforeseen occurs. If a client comes out of nowhere with a crazy panic because they are the most important in the world, always add a fee for speed, clarifying the time it takes you in normal time for similar works, which you'll make an exception for them. Normally, these prices vary between 50% or 100% of the labor price. It is best to avoid these sorts of jobs as you begin to get used to the client, only accept these cases if it's strictly necessary.

Minimum Price

You have heard the expression "I am not going to get out of bed for less than 1,000 pesos per hour." That is what we have to calculate. What hourly rate makes the project worth your time, energy, and knowledge, additionally to cover any expenses or wear and tear on your supplies?

If someone asks you to do a small job, like "write my name," you would like to be prepared together with your minimum load. Sure, you will not charge her a price per name on the invitation (say $ 50) and they would leave like that.

Taking under consideration the time it will take to contact so-and-so for details (style, color, size, delivery, etc.), the time required to assemble your materials, and to organize your workspace (remove the dishes from the dining room table, for example, and send or deliver the final piece, $ 50 isn't close to covering your time, energy and materials).

CHAPTER 7

MOST REQUESTED PROJECTS

Custom T-Shirts

Have you ever wondered how custom T-shirts are made? Well, you are not the only one, as most people are suckers for such apparel. If you would like to make some T-shirts for yourself, then I have great news for you: they are quite easy to make using the proper technology on your Cricut machine. You heard me, right! These T-shirts are often created using one of the most common and basic Cricut materials: iron-on vinyl. The method also can be called heat transfer vinyl (aka HTV).

This is the right option to wear your T-shirts or on adorable baby bodysuits. So, let's start with your requirements.

For this project, you can need:

- Cricut Explore (any model) or Cricut Maker.
- Cricut iron-on vinyl.
- Bodysuit or a T-shirt.
- Green standard grip mat or a blue light grip mat.
- A weeding tool.
- Cricut easy press, a heat press, or an iron piece of cloth of a minimum of 9" x 9" (but this is often optional)
- Files from Cricut access with text and models of your choice.

Directions

First, you will need to open the Cricut design space to use images from the library, so attend the planning panel from the left side and click on Images. Look for very interesting images that you think would work very nicely with your T-shirt. Once the files are opened in Canvas, you can resize them using the edit toolbar (located at the top). You can prefer to increase the size a bit on the pictures you chose. To avoid any material waste, use the color sync panel (from the top left corner of the layers panel) to tug and drop images on the same layer to seem on the same color. If they appear in the same color, they are going to be cut on the same mat.

When you are satisfied with the top result, click the Make it button from the top side of the Canvas. You can then see the preview screen. Importantly, in this screen, you will need to click "mirror" in the sidebar to flip the image, or the image will be shown backward when you want to iron it. When you see the slider on the left green and the project exposure backward on the mat, you recognize that the settings are right. Please click "continue," and when you get to the make screen, you will need to connect your Cricut machine. From the society dial (for Explore machines), select Iron-on; if you are using Cricut maker, select the Iron-on material from the list. The blade you will be using for this cut is that the fine-point blade.

Once the cut is completed, you can press the arrow key and the Cricut machine will release your mat. This is often when you have to use the Cricut weeding tool, as you will need to remove anything that is not a part of your project. First, you will need to dig your weeding tool's tip into a vinyl piece that is not a part of your design and pull it up gently. When you have a good chunk of vinyl that is not supposed to be there, you can also use your fingers, but remember to use the weeding tool for more complicated bits (these include the insides of letters as well). Still, remove all the bits from the side until only the image remains. If you flip the design, you will see that the image is facing the proper way.

Make sure you double-check your work, as you don't want anything unwanted after the weeding process.

Then, you will need to adhere to the Cricut iron-on vinyl. If you have Cricut easy press, that is great, but bear in mind that you can use an easy iron or heat press. Let's say that you don't have an easy press device or any heat press. In this case, you can just use a clear iron. Ensure that the iron basin is totally empty, as you don't want steam on your iron-on. Before you place the iron-on the T-shirt, do a pre-press with the iron for about 5 seconds. This pre-press will ensure that the iron reaches a really high temperature. There is no steam remaining. It can help flatten the onesie and start adhesion once you add the decal.

When you start the ironing process, it is highly recommended to use a bit of cotton on top of the plastic carrier sheet. You don't want to melt the carrier sheet, so this is often why it is better to do it in this manner. Plus, there will not be any uneven heating. Make sure you depress the iron, hold it down firmly for around 15 to 30 seconds, then pick it up and move it if the image gets larger than your iron. DON'T SLIDE THE IRON!!!

Let the decal cool as the vinyl adhesive takes longer to set. It is like if you cold peel vinyl, and you give the vinyl adhesive a longer time to set, the top result is going to be simply amazing.

This is when you will need to pull back the plastic carrier sheet from the rear of your image. Normally, the vinyl should stick, but if it doesn't, put the plastic carrier back on and apply more heat.

Tip: press with your iron at the very best heat (don't ditch the piece of cotton) for at least 10 more seconds, flip your project over, and press the iron again (still using the piece of cotton) for around 15 seconds. Then, you can remove the entire plastic and the vinyl should remain.

You can do this process with different apparel, from T-shirts to baby bodysuits. Don't expect to succeed on your first attempt, as you will need to do that a couple of times until you catch on right. Doing such projects on clothes is often very easy once you get the hang of it. These projects are very practical and popular. You can make a lot of money from such projects, and the better part is that you really don't need to invest too much.

Vinyl Crafts

As we have mentioned in this book earlier, vinyl is a super beginner-friendly material to work with and comes in various colors and patterns to add to its great reputation. You can create customized labels for glass containers and canisters to help anyone looking to organize their pantry. Explore the online trends and adjust the labels.

Once you have your labels designed, the easiest approach is to set up an Etsy shop, which is free and very easy to use. It's almost like opening an Amazon prime membership account. If your design is in demand, you will have people ordering even with no advertising. But if you would like to keep the tempo high, then advertise your Etsy listing on Pinterest and other social media platforms. This is a sure-shot way to generate more traffic to your Etsy shop and turning potential customers into paying customers. An important note here is the pictures being used on your listing. You cannot use any of the stock images from the design space application and must use your pictures that match the product you are selling.

Create a package of 5 or 6 different labels like sugar, salt, rice, oats, beans, etc. That can be sold as a standard packager and offer a customized package that will allow the customer to request any word they need be included in their set. Since these labels weigh next to nothing, shipping can easily be managed with standard mail with usually only a single postage stamp, depending on the delivery address. Make sure you do not claim the next day or two-day delivery for these.

Build enough delivery time so you can create and ship the labels without any stress. Once you have an established business model, you can adjust the price and shipping of your product, but more on that later. Check out other Etsy listings to make sure your product pricing is competitive enough, and you are attracting enough potential buyers.

Now, once you have traction in the market, you can offer additional vinyl-based projects like bumper stickers, iron-on, or heat transfer vinyl designs that people can transfer on their clothing using a standard heating iron.

Once you have gained some clientele, you can modify and customize all your listings to develop into a one-stop-shop for all things vinyl (great name for your future Etsy shop, right!).

CHAPTER 8

LEARN TO TAKE ADVANTAGE OF TRENDS (CHRISTMAS, HALLOWEEN, KIDS' WORLD TOYS/CARTOON)

Special Occasion Projects

Chipboard Tree Ornaments

Personalized Christmas ornaments are filled with history and memories for a family. With the Cricut, you can make all sorts of Christmas tree ornaments. Once you have mastered the art of making them, get the family involved in decorating them.

Materials:

- Cricut glitter adhesive vinyl—red or a selection of colors.
- Cricut chipboard.
- Green standard grip mat.
- Purple strong grip map.
- Knife blade.
- Weeding tool.
- Spatula.
- Pair of scissors for cutting.
- Ribbon—red or white.
- White matte finish paint.
- Builder's tape.

Steps:

1. Open a new project in the design space.
2. Select "diamond" from the shapes menu on the left-hand side.
3. Leave the color as the default color.
4. Unlock the shape and change it to 1.969" wide and 3.416" long.
5. Select "octagon" from the shapes menu on the left-hand side.
6. Leave it as the default color.

7. Leave the shape as the default 3.111" wide and 3.111" long.

8. Select "star" from the shapes menu on the left-hand side.

9. Leave color as the default color.

10. Leave the shape as the default 3.271" wide and 3.111" long.

11. Select "heart" from the shapes menu on the left-hand side.

12. Leave the shape as the default 3.282" wide and 3.106" long.

13. Select "text" from the menu on the left-hand side.

14. Choose a nice Christmas font. Balega STD regular is used as an example for this project. The font size is set to 44.2.

15. Type "peace" and move the text to the middle of the octagon. Leave some space on either side of the text box.

16. Duplicate the text and move the duplicate text to one side out of the way.

17. Highlight the text and octagon, right-click, and select "slice."

18. Remove the top 2 slices and delete them.

19. Repeat steps 17 to 20 for each shape.

20. Type "love" for the heart shape.

21. Type "joy" for the star shape.

22. Type "hope" for the diamond shape.

23. Select "circle" from the shapes menu on the left-hand side.

24. Leave the color as the default color.

25. Leave the shape as the default 0.306" wide and 0.306" long.

26. Make four duplicates of the small circle.

27. Position one circle on the left round part of the heart shape.

28. Select the circle and the heart, right-click, and select "slice."

29. Remove and delete the top 2 slices.

30. Repeat steps 26 to 28 for the right round part of the heart shape.

31. Position one circle on the top point of the star shape.

32. Select the circle and the star, right-click, and select "slice."

33. Remove then delete the top 2 slices.

34. Repeat steps 30 to 32 for the rest of the shapes, positioning the circle at the top in the middle of each.

35. Click "make it."

36. You can fit at least 2 of each shape onto one board.

37. Set project copies to 2 and click "apply."

38. Position the objects on the page so they are not touching.

39. Set the Cricut blade to the fine-point blade and print out the glitter vinyl copies first.

40. Each ornament will need two vinyl overlays, one for each side. It is suggested to have one side in red glitter vinyl and the other side in green glitter vinyl.

41. Once the glitter vinyl copies have finished cutting, set the Cricut blade to the knife blade and use the purple mat.

42. Remember to stick the chipboard down with builder's tape to keep it steady.

43. While the chipboard is being cut, weed the vinyl overlays and get them ready.

44. When the chipboard has finished being cut, remove the ornaments from the mat.

45. Clean the shapes and text.

46. Paint them on both sides and the edges with the white matte or chalk finish paint.

47. Leave the ornaments to dry completely.

48. When the ornaments are dry, carefully transfer the glitter vinyl onto them.

49. Cut pieces of ribbon and tie them through the little holes on the top of the ornaments.

50. They are ready to hang on the tree.

Valentine's Gift Tags

In a few steps, you can create this easy-I-love-you gift with Cricut. Make a donation tag or stack. I have a canvas of design space, click and create.

You can customize the Valentine Cricut project's look by replacing your cutting materials, selecting your favorite colors to go with a fun fabric. You can also flatten the entire design piece into a multitude of Cricut Projects print-then-cut.

Materials:

- Cricut machine design space.
- Account variety of card inventory.
- Gold pen.
- Cut designs you need to create this I love you gift tag with your Cricut.

Steps:

1. Follow on-screen instructions to draw and cut each layer as required.
2. Glue the two layers of paper together, aligning the heart-shaped hole atop the tag.
3. Add the vinyl and burn to guarantee it adheres carefully. I can't apply vinyl, particularly glitter vinyl. You can attempt using the transfer tape, but the glitter tends not to stick to the transfer tape.
4. Add twine or ribbon to the tag and attach the tag as you like. You can use the title back to write a unique signal to someone.
5. Alternatively, instead of using glue, you can bind the two cutouts together. Add these Valentine tags in your charms, embellishments, and fun accents.
6. Draw a beautiful accent design with your gold glitter pen. Add glitter vinyl word art to your Valentine tag.
7. You can use this pleasant Valentine's Day Cricut project to produce all kinds of custom tags or use parts to make other types of projects. Change colors, materials, and wording.

Halloween T-Shirt

Materials:

- T-shirt blanks.

- Glam Halloween SVG files.

- Cardstock.

- Transfer sheets (black and pink).

- Butcher paper (comes with Infusible ink rolls).

Steps:

1. Import the SVG files into the Cricut design space and arrange them as you want them on the T-shirt.

2. Change the sizes of the designs to get them to fit on the T-shirt.

3. Using the slice tool, slice the pink band away from the hat's bowler part (the largest piece). Please make a copy of this band, and then cut it from the lower part of the hat. With these done, you will have three pieces that fit together.

4. You can change the designs' colors as you would like them. When you are done with the preparation, click "make it."

5. Ensure that you invert your image using the "mirror" toggle. This is even more important if there is text on your design, as infusible ink designs should be done in inverse. This is because the part with the ink is to go right on the destination material.

6. For the material, select infusible ink. After this, cut the design out using your Cricut machine.

7. With the designs cut out, weed the transfer sheet.

8. Cut around the designs such that the transfer tape does not cover any part of the infusible ink sheet. Make sure that this is done well as any part of the infusible ink that is not in contact with the fabric will not be transferred.

9. Preheat your easy press to 385°, and set your easy press mat.

10. Prepare your T-shirt by placing it on the easy press mat, then using a lint roller to remove any lint from the front.

11. Insert the cardstock in the t-shirt, between the front and back, just where the design will be. This will protect the other side of the T-shirt from having infusible ink on it.

12. To layer colors, ensure that you're cutting around the transfer sheet is done as close as possible, then repeat the previous three steps for each color. This will prevent the transfer sheet from removing part of the paint on the previously transferred design.

No-Sew Felt Nativity Finger Puppets

Utilize your Cricut Creator to make this charming no-sew felt nativity finger manikins.

On the off chance that you don't have kids of your own, I think these would influence a fantastic Christmas to present for neighbors with kids or grandchildren.

Materials:

- Cricut producer.

- Rotary edge (accompanies Cricut producer).

- Cricut felt sky sampler.

- Cricut felt a merry-go-round sampler.

- Cricut fabric grip tangle.

- Hot stick weapon and paste sticks.

Steps:

1. Open Cricut configuration space and open this record —> Nativity finger manikins.

2. Click on "make it" and select "felt" as the material to cut. Load your rotational edge into your machine and load the relating shade of felt that appeared on the outline screen onto your Cricut fabric grip tangle.

3. Once you have removed the majority of your mats, precisely amass every one of the manikins together to get together.

4. Using your heated glue weapon, make a line of paste around the back of the finger manikin. Lay the front piece to finish everything and press to anchor. At that point stick the other manikin pieces, for example, hair, face, and arms on. Rehash with every manikin. You will dependably complete a finger molded line of paste on the back bit of the manikin.

5. Presently your manikins are finished! Give those little fingers a chance to play away with their own nativity.

CHAPTER 9

TIPS AND TRICKS TO IMPROVE SALES AND BOOST MY BUSINESS

Alright, now that we have obtained that legal things out of the way, let us discuss the way to really make money with your Cricut!

Narrow Your Cricut Craft Niche

Among the worst things you can do is choose to make whatever folks ask one to create. A tumbler here, a house decor hint there, birthday t-shirts then. You are going to wind up with lower margins and wasted merchandise, along with a confused crowd. Instead, narrow your product down to one or two things or topics, and then nail it. I suggest choosing something in the junction of everything you love to create and what's rewarding (see below for pricing thoughts.) You wish to appreciate what you are creating—and you would like it to be worth your time.

When you are trying to decide what things to create and market along with your Cricut, think about "added value," this may include both enhancements to a product, or actually niching down. This way you may charge a premium for your goods.

A lot of people are making home-made hints, for example, possibly your "item" is adding paper succulents or hand-painted glitter accents. Perhaps, you hand letter and flip your decoration into stickers for tops. If you are making tumblers, perhaps they're specifically targeted to teachers and have a gift cardholder. Perhaps your onesie store is filled with cute things, especially for preemies.

If you are among the only people doing something, you are able to charge more! It also makes it much easier to target your advertisements.

For you to become successful in the Cricut world of crafts, you have to keep the following in mind:

Dare to Be Different

You have to be yourself, unleash your quirkiness and creativity. Those that have been in the Cricut crafts world for some time know all about the knockout name tiles. They became a hit, and in no time, everyone was producing and selling them.

In the crafting world, that is the norm. Thus, you could be among the earliest people to jump on a trend to ride the wave until the following hot seller surfaces. Mind you, that strategy of selling Cricut crafts can become costly and tiresome if you are not careful.

Take out time to think about your area of strength and focus your energy on making products that you'd be known for. It is better to be known as an expert in a particular product than to be renowned as someone that produces a high number of inferior products.

Thus, you should keep it narrow and grow to become the very best in your area of craft.

Be Consistent

If you intend to become successful, you have to work on your Cricut craft business consistently. Some people work once a week, or thereabout because they sell as a hobby; however, if you intend to make in-road in your business, you have to work every day.

If you have other engagements and can't work every day, then you should create a weekly schedule and stick to it. If you shun your business for weeks and months at a time, then you will not go anywhere with it. Thus, for you to be successful in your craft, you have to be tenacious and resilient. Be willing to maneuver your way through tough times, and do not forget to pick up lessons.

Quality Control

If you intend to grow your brand, you must prioritize the selling of high-quality products. Your motto should say "quality over everything."

For you to easily succeed, people should know you as someone that sells top-quality products, because quality wins over quantity every day of the week. You don't want to be known as someone that produces poor-quality items because when the word spreads (and it surely will), your business will pack up.

If you focus your attention and efforts on the production of high-quality materials, you will be able to withstand competition, no matter how stiff it is.

Before we reach a number of the best items to create and market with a Cricut, let us cover a few commonly asked questions concerning promoting Cricut jobs and starting a craft business.

Purchase Materials in Bulk

If you have nailed down your market, you can purchase your materials and supplies in bulk. You're able to purchase more tumblers or eyeglasses or vinyl at a more affordable price if you purchase in bulk. If you are still making "one-off" items, it is far more difficult to keep in bulk. If you are making holiday t-shirts, as an example, rather than purchasing routine rolls of iron vinyl in a craft shop, you can purchase in bulk to lower prices.

Just as the Cricut machine can be used in a million and one ways, the ways to generate money from it are also numerous.

Some of the ways to generate money from the Cricut machine are highlighted below:

Make and Sell Leather Bracelets

Bracelets are fashionable items, especially leather bracelets. The Cricut machine can easily cut real or faux leather, giving you less work to do. If you decide to cut, make, and sell leather bracelets, know that the materials needed are just snaps: your Cricut machine, leather, and probably card stock.

If you are interested in selling this craft, you can also create room for preordering, where a buyer can order for a particular design to be created by the designer.

Sell Stickers

This idea is targeted at kids. You can make money by designing educative and entertaining stickers for toddlers and other age groups. Stickers of the alphabet or a map of a locale can be made. Stickers are also used in decorating places like the wardrobe or closets.

Make and Sell Party Decorations and Buntings

There is always a celebration in our day-to-day lives as human beings. It can be a milestone celebration, or simply a fun-seeking escapade. Party decorations made with the Cricut machine can be sold on these occasions.

Window Decals

Everyone has a peculiar image; an object we are practically obsessed with. Getting a vinyl window decal of one's favorite image will go a long way in giving your decor a boost. Making and selling window decals is quite easy and profitable.

Design and Sell Leather Neck Piece

The leather pendant can be designed for a necklace and sold out to interested buyers. An all-leather neckpiece can also be made and sold.

Design and Sell Banners

Banners can be made for celebrations, festive periods, camping, parties, religious activities, or sporting activities. All these can be made and sold.

Design and Sell Stencils

Stencils can be created and sold for those that want to hand-paint a post or sign. It would also generate a nice amount of money.

Design and Sell Safari Animal Stickers

Stickers of safari animals are attractive items. They can be sold to animal lovers. Stickers are easy to make, and will also be a source of income generation.

Design and Sell Christmas Ornaments

Christmas is a period people celebrate and decorate their workplace, abode, and religious settings, among others.

Design and Sell Doormats

A beautiful doormat can be made with the machine and sold to customers. It can be designed with either text or images.

Design and Sell Kitchen Towels

Towels used in the kitchen can be designed and sold at affordable prices. The towels can be designed with text or images of delicacies. There are countless things you can make with Cricut. Likewise, there are countless things you can make, which are marketable. Independent entrepreneurship is easier than it's ever been thanks to the internet and web platforms that make selling your products a breeze. You've likely already heard of some of the platforms that make it easy to start a shop of your own. Etsy is probably the most well-known of these platforms and setting up a shop with them is so simple, it's almost impossible not to be interested in starting one for yourself!

Tips and Tricks

Stockpile on Crafting Materials

Stockpiling on materials is especially recommended if you are planning to advance your skills, as you will surely do a lot of test cutting as you are getting familiar with different types of materials and designs you can make with the Cricut machine and design space. Make sure to try out as many different materials as possible when planning your projects. This will help you learn how to pick materials for your future projects based on what you are planning to make with your Cricut.

You don't have to stockpile in big quantities, although, you can find better prices for materials when buying in bulk orders online. This will also help you save some money you could later use for additional tools or your savings account. Aside from investing in crafting materials, you should consider investing in Cricut access, or in different patterns and images you could use for your designs. However, you can also find a lot of free to download SVG files, you can then upload them to the design space and use them for your projects. Be ready and make sure to have everything you need, so you can act in no time whenever you feel like crafting something new.

Editing and Designing

Editing and designing are the core of your skillfulness with Cricut design space. You can always upload ready-to-make designs and patterns and make a few edits as possible (e.g., resizing and arranging proportions) before submitting your design for cutting. You can always upload ready-to-make designs and patterns and make as few edits as possible (e.g., resizing and arranging proportions) before submitting your design for cutting. However, an advanced crafter knows their way around editing and designing tools. An advanced crafter is not afraid to use pens and blades likewise and they do not hesitate to try out available tools and commands available in the design space. Whenever you are in doubt, you can get back to book one and go through in-depth guidelines on different parts of the Cricut software and Canvas (commands, tools, features, templates, image library, etc.) You can challenge yourself to use more editing and designing tools in Canvas while exploring all possibilities the design space has to offer.

Project Planning

We have collected dozens of interesting designs and projects for Cricut machines, and the design space for you to practice as a beginner, advanced crafter, and a crafter ready to start working on Cricut designs as a professional. The internet (a vast never-ending space with endless sources of information) is where you can find tons of different projects for the Cricut machine, also for free. However, in case you want to advance in your skills and become a professional Cricut crafter, you need to be able to come up with your projects and ideas. Don't be afraid to experiment, as you can make all kinds of projects with Cricut. Pay attention to "templates" in the design space and see what sorts of templates are offered in the library, you might get inspired when you see a scope of all kinds of projects one can make with Cricut. Browsing through templates may help you plan a project. You can always start by drafting your designs and looking for inspiration.

CHAPTER 10

HOW I CAN MAKE MARKETING CORRECTLY

Okay, I know you want to like just quit your job. Only gain financial freedom, enough time to spend with your family and your friends, or make just enough to go traveling or you want to build, well, I don't know if I could help you create a $1 billion business. Still, there are a lot of million-dollar trades that get made online all the time. You can even start selling your products as a side-hustle while you're still working. And then, if you are successful, you may be able to turn it into your full-time job. So, whatever it is, set that intention and know that just if you work hard enough, you don't give up; I bet you can do that. And this is the best business opportunity to do that right now in history. Yeah, I'll let you work hard, but Cricut is mainly fun, so don't forget to have a lot of fun with it.

So, I'm going to tell you all the roadblocks that stop most sellers and then how you guys can get past them. Just exponential growth and that's what will happen to you. But you need to take care of yourself. Every single bit of that process is what was required for that tree to grow.

You have to be able to get inside the mind of your potential customer. Remember, especially online, the two things you got are your product and your listing. Online, remember the only thing you got is your listing. They can't touch, feel, taste your product, none of that. It's all just those photos in those descriptions and, sooner or later, reviews. So, you got to put all your effort and time into those when you get started.

Your Cricut Business through the Digital World

In today's day and age, if you are not advertising on the Internet, you are losing a significant amount of business. It doesn't matter if you are going to be Cricut savvy or not. It would help if you found your way to be online anyway.

By taking advantage of the internet, you allow your business to grow in ways that it could not if you were to advertise with conventional methods.

As with any new business, do you need to do some research? Let me tell you that you are in advantage compared to the other online beginners because you know which direction you are taking; you want to work with your Cricut! It is much easier to manage a store or anything online related to your interests; it cannot deny.

Attention, I am not saying that it is not possible to do it inside a niche that you do not know or that does not represent your direct passion, for example, if you can't work woods with your Cricut. You are more passionate about creating intangible files; indeed, it will be a bit more complicated because you must use the materials and react to the design.

It is because if you know about the topic covered in your niche, you will be able to more easily recognize the elements of value to offer to your potential customers. The more specific and specialized you are, the more you win over your competitors.

You will be able to identify the best products to market using qualitative and high-level descriptions. And don't think you are limited because you are using your Cricut. It is not a professional tool because with it and coordinating with some local professionals like a carpenter or a tailor, you can create many tangible and intangible items that result in being very professional and good-looking.

You will be able to answer even the most technical and complex questions your customers will ask you, and it will be much easier to identify all the elements to be used to get a better grip on the public.

So, go with this practical step by step essential guide to start your business and not quit until you made it.

Marketing Your Cricut Business

The more you know about your target audience, the more you know where to put the market. By breaking down the different groups, we can sell and understand where to find them in local and internet-based sales, you can determine the best way to put your precious time and energy. If you decide to be a local seller, it's best to choose between one of these two segments.

Focus on one of those above, spend your energy in one that, and results will come soon. If you decide to provide custom works, please do not try to become a dashboard simultaneously after establishing an initial foothold and obtaining considerable sales.

Business to Business

The opportunities are fewer, and client expectations are higher. So, for this reason, I recommend starting an easy path.

Another thing to consider is accounting; if you are a top creative but lacking, you need to take very carefully in your business strategy. Unfortunately, one of the top reasons most businesses fail is managing finances and their inferior accounting methods. You might consider investing part of your money in buying accounting software that can help you with that. There are a few affordable tools that you can find online to keep track of your expenses.

Phase 1

1. Think and write down your plan of action. There is no path for those who don't have a clue where they are going.

The first things you need to determine are:

- What kind of product you are going to sell.
- What type of customers are you going to reach?
- How you are going to find them.

For example, you want to sell customized woods for little coffee shops or small farms. You don't want to take the risk, so it is better to test your local area to see how it goes.

2. Search about your competitors.

- What are your competitor's top-selling products?
- How much they charge for their products.
- What channels (online or offline, or both) your competitors are using for marketing.
- Find out where your competitors are lacking.

You need to take your time and do marketing research about your competitor's success and its products.

Phase 2

Cost of materials.

1. Make sure the cost of material is actually at a bare minimum.

- Consider all the activities involved, which includes manufacturing, purchasing, and delivery.

- The quality of the material and the final product must be high enough to satisfy the customer need.

- There are going to be some unused scraps and material when buying in bulk.

Phase 3

Who do you sell to? What should you sell? Where can you sell it?

I know that you are excited to start selling your products, but it is essential to take responsible steps before starting. Many of your business decisions will depend on the target audience, so you must first determine the target audience. For example, if your business idea is to create menu boards, your possible target audience can be restaurants or coffee shops in your city.

Phase 4

Testing your business.

You don't want to create a product that no one wants to buy; otherwise, your time, money, and resources will be wasted entirely.

If you want to succeed in your business, you need to take responsible steps, and you can test the market to see if people will want to buy what you plan to sell. So, give some try by producing a few prototypes to offer your unique products to potential buyers and see how they react.

24 Goal Ideas for Craft Businesses

2. Financial.

3. $xx in weeks' / month revenues.

4. Reduce your business expenses.

5. Keep business accounting up to date.

6. Make your company a city, state, or county official. While I can't tell you precisely how to do this, there's an excellent starting point here—different in every country.

7. Keep purchasing impulses at a minimum in your company. In this post, read more about cash wasters.

8. Pay off the debts of your company and avoid liability. Debt is no good—see how you can keep your company out.

9. Set up a company savings account automatically draft your company bank account.

10. Post to social media regularly.

11. Create and begin using a profile on a new social media network.

12. Start with a calendar of content. In this article, I have more info on these calendars.

13. Network to encourage your goods jointly with other tiny company owners.

14. Begin marketing for a new population. If you are presently producing goods mainly for mothers, broaden your marketing to include other groups of individuals.

15. Get out of the market and launch your website.

16. Buy a loyalty program for your clients.

17. Note that you have the most straightforward client to get! It is my loyalty sample program.

18. Enhance your branding. You may have your logo, brand colors, packaging, etc.

19. Register for a course related to business.

20. I often hear from owners of small businesses that "my product photos are bad." Make it a better objective!

21. Contact your customers more to find out what they want. Whether social media or surveys, the best product is that which meets your requirements.

22. Start something new.

23. If you produce and sell wood signs, consider hosting guests, too. At this link, pick up my 15-party eBook.

24. Create pop-up stores all year round to increase your company knowledge. Think of how many people you might attend for the year when you set a target—a month? A quarter by one?

Conclusion

Congratulations on making it to the end.

Anything you can create with your own hands can inspire others. Any beautifully handcrafted item you produce using your Cricut machine has a different value. And this could be the start of something new. It can boost your self-esteem and relieve stress. Give you the chance to be in touch with your inner self and allow yourself to express yourself.

Remember not to be under pressure to create something big. You are still in the early stages. So, in the beginning, try to make as many projects as possible. This way you can gain more experience and better understand all the possibilities of your new machine. You'll have more time to experiment and try out larger-scale projects once you know the basics. Enjoy.

CPSIA information can be obtained
at www.ICGtesting.com
Printed in the USA
BVHW090945030721
610976BV00020B/385